# CINNIA'S STORY

# CINNIA'S STORY

A Story about Family, War Survival,
Career, Life, and Love

## LILY VIOLET

Library of Congress Control Number:    2017906460
ISBN:           Hardcover              978-1-5434-0047-2
                Softcover              978-1-5434-0046-5
                eBook                  978-1-5434-0045-8

Print information available on the last page.

Rev. date: 05/01/2017

**To order additional copies of this book, contact:**
Xlibris
1-800-455-039
www.Xlibris.com.au
Orders@Xlibris.com.au
756799

# CONTENTS

I dedicate this book to you.

No matter how hard life seems, you

should never give up on yourself.

# PROLOGUE

This is my life story written for anyone who is going through hard times in life—a story about family, war survival, career, life struggles, love, hope, and miracles.

I wrote this book as a way of healing myself after everything I have gone through. Putting everything on paper has given me one last time to reflect on how far I have come in life and all the things I should feel grateful for.

I wrote it in hopes that my story will help and inspire people. Know that you are not alone. We cannot control our lives or what happens to us, but we can choose to believe in ourselves, we can choose not to give up when it gets hard, and we can accept that we are broken but rise stronger and wiser. It is up to us to invest in ourselves and to never lose goodness in our hearts.

Everything that happens in our lives occurs to teach us something and show us our true strength; it is up to us how we perceive it.

This is my life, my story, my heart and soul.

CHAPTER 1

# LIFE BEFORE WAR

I arrived in this world in July 1987 as the firstborn to a happy young family. My father was twenty-nine years old, and my mother was twenty-two. They had had some trouble conceiving me, so my arrival was a little miracle. The first years of my young life were filled with love, happiness, and blessings. Everyone says I was too young to remember, but sometimes, memories of those years come to me in my dreams, when I hear a song or have a piece of fruit, or when we talk about certain situations. I remember everything.

Soon after I turned two years of age, we welcomed my little brother into our family. I will never forget that feeling I had the first time I saw him. His arms, fingers, and feet were so small. I promised him I would always protect him. By the time Mother was out of the hospital, Father and I had everything ready for us to move into our own home. They had been building it ever since I was born. I was only twenty-eight months old, but I did my share of picking furniture for our home. Father took me everywhere with him.

That first night sleeping in our new home felt so special because I could remember Mother and Father only going to our property every day after work, so I rarely got to spend time with them. They stayed so busy, building our perfect little house. Moving in as one happy family felt amazing. We finally had our home. Everything looked really pretty, Mother and Father looked happy, and I had plenty of time to play after work, which I loved the most.

April 1991 is one of the most memorable times of my life. One day, Mother and Father were having coffee after work while I played under the dining table with my brother. He was very little and could not speak or understand what I said to him, but I still played with him. We were having an imaginary lunch, and I tried to explain to him that he could not eat the coins that I had given to him but that he should pretend that they were his lunch. He was about eighteen months old, and I was almost four years old. And I was clueless about how dangerous my game was.

Suddenly, when I looked at my brother, I saw he was completely blue and had red eyes. He was choking on one of the coins. I started screaming and got him out from under the table. My mother jumped and screamed. My father took my brother by his little legs and started swinging him around, head down, trying to get the blockage out of him. At that time, they did not know I fed him coins. They just knew he was choking on something.

Soon enough, they called an ambulance, but my father carried my little brother to the car and started driving towards the hospital so he could get help sooner. All I can remember from the moment my father left was the look on my mother's face and her words: "You have killed my son." I do not remember that night or anything else that happened.

The next day, my father called from the hospital, saying that my brother was alive and well. Doctors and nurses had to remove a coin from his windpipe, but we were blessed that the coin stayed straight all that time. If it had moved, he would have died. I felt so relieved that he was healthy and coming home. I loved him so much. He was everything to me.

## CHAPTER 2

# LIFE DURING WAR

In early spring of 1992, something happened. My mother and father looked so worried every day. My brother and I stopped getting sweet treats when they came home from work. There was no more going out on our adventures or any kind of shopping. My parents started arguing. That really surprised me, as I had never seen them talk like that to each other. Father kept saying that we wouldn't have any money left, as "they" (the banks) had stopped all transactions and there was no money to take. He said Mother was supposed to have saved prior to this big mess. I did not understand what a big mess was, but I was about to.

One very dark night, all our neighbours gathered in our home, and for the very first time, I heard, "War has started." I remember sitting in the corner of our living room with the rest of the little kids, some of them my cousins. No one seemed worried by the fact that grown-ups were talking about war. We were all about the same age, but they kept eating our treats and playing with our dolls. I did not like that. I sneaked to my bedroom and started packing my backpack, books, pyjamas, a few pairs of underwear, socks, a jumper, and toys.

After everyone left and my brother was asleep, I asked my parents what it meant now that war had started. "Where will we go?"

Father looked at me and said, "We will think of something, but for now, go to sleep. Tomorrow, we will have to pack and will move." I started crying and said that I had packed my stuff already. I was scared. Every time I closed my eyes, I could see monsters, and I kept crying.

Morning came very fast. I guess I hadn't slept much. I kept thinking about what would happen to us. My father's plan was to get my mother, my brother, and me to a safe city, as ours would soon be under attack. Mother packed a few bags, and we got on the bus with other families to a different country. We were welcomed in a small city and got accommodations in an abandoned childcare centre. Luckily, in our group, my mother, my brother, and I; my mother's sister and her children; and my grandmother were on the same bus, so we did not feel as alone as some other families felt. Unfortunately, Father and the rest of the family had to stay in our country.

Days were long and hot. All we could see on the television were lists of dead people and our cities being destroyed. My mother and aunty worked all day long, cleaning, picking fruit and vegetables, or doing any decent job that would provide food. Some days, they would get paid in fruit, some days in vegetables, and some days in milk or eggs. We received help from the Red Cross, including basic hygiene products, flour, and oil.

We were never hungry. Grandmother would bake fresh bread every morning and make something to eat it with. She was like another mother to the five of us grandchildren, since Mother and Aunty were too tired or emotionally drained to mind us or give us much attention. Some nights were so hard that Mother would cry and cry and call Father's name in her dreams. It was horrible. She did not look like herself anymore. She lost so much weight and always had swollen eyes from crying. She rarely played with my brother and me or talked to us.

And then one day, we received a call from back home that my grandfather, Mother's father, had been killed. That moment was unforgettable—screams, tears, swearing, and the looks in their eyes, and so much pain. Throughout everything that happened, I always tried to protect my brother so he didn't have to see any of the nightmares we were going through.

A few months passed, and the war heated up even more. Every night at 7:30 p.m., we watched the news to see what was going on and who had died—maybe someone we knew—as it always had a list of casualties. Then one night, it happened; our city was under attack, and that night, we saw my father on the dead list, right there in front of our eyes on the television.

For a second, everyone was quiet. Mother was in absolute shock. She screamed so loudly that the whole street could hear her. Soon enough, our neighbours came to see us. They tried to calm her down, to tell her that it might be a mistake and that she had two young children so she needed her sanity. Nope, she did not listen. She started walking around the backyard smoking cigarettes—she never smoked before—and pulling her hair like an insane person. It was a horrible, horrible, horrible night.

As for me, I put my brother to sleep, and then all I said about my father to my grandmother was that he had not died. I knew he was alive because I could feel him in my heart. I am crying as I write this, remembering everything, including looking at my mother, completely broken after losing the love of her life. I remember every scream, every tear, that little hand of mine on my heart, and that little voice saying, "Father is not dead. He is still alive. I can feel him here." I did not cry that night, or for many years after.

The morning was even worse. Mother was close to a nervous breakdown, and no one could do anything to help her. We did not have medical help or money to take her to a hospital, so my grandmother kept making more chamomile tea to calm her down. By that afternoon, Mother had made her mind up about taking us back home. She argued to my grandmother that if my father was dead, as people on television had said, she wanted us all to die, including her, my brother, and me, because she could not imagine her life without my father. She organised tickets in the next few days, and in a week, we were on the bus back home.

The ride was terrible and very long. It was so hot and smelly. I was so hungry and sick most of the time. We had no place to sit, even though my mother paid for three full tickets. It was packed. A lady, who had two of her little children sitting on two seats, offered to my mother that I could sit in one, as I looked so sick. Every few minutes, I would turn around and see my mother sitting on the floor of the bus, holding my brother in her arms. I felt bad about sitting in a seat, so after a few minutes, I ran to my mother and said that I felt so much better and would like to sit with her.

Oops, I am tearing up again. I guess it doesn't matter how old you are or how well you think you have healed; you can never erase those feelings you felt. You can replay the whole situation in your mind as if it happened a second ago. I will never forget that smell, the heat, all those people, and the many, many, many tears. I will never forget the way my mother looked sitting on the floor of that old bus, holding my brother.

After so many hours of driving, we arrived in our city. We were informed that the electricity and water had been cut and the bus driver wouldn't do drop-offs, as it was too dangerous. He would just stop at the main station, and we would all be on our own. Mother explained to me that it would be very dark but she knew the way to the place where we would stay and that I shouldn't feel scared; everything would be fine. Mind you, this was coming from a woman who said she wanted to go back to a war zone to die with her children, so you will understand that I was a little bit iffy on the whole "everything will be fine" story.

And then a miracle happened. As my mother exited the bus, holding my hand and my brother in her arms, someone called her name. A male person called her name, asking if it was her. It was so dark. The city was dead; all the light we had came from the bus, so you can imagine the visibility. We could not even see one metre ahead. And then she said my father's name for the first time since she had seen his name on that list on TV. She screamed my father's name and said, "You are alive! You are alive! And I came here to die, so we could be together."

Let me remind you my father's name was on the casualties list, and everyone thought that he had died—everyone except me. To this day, I think that is the most romantic and craziest story ever, but let me tell more you about how crazy and connected my parents are.

So that night, when we had seen Father's name on the casualties list, yes, he had been under attack, but luckily, he was the one who survived. He walked for kilometres to get to a hospital, as he was badly injured. He saw his name on the list, but no telephones worked to let my mother know that he was alive. So he had waited for the bus every night at the station, because he knew how crazy my mother was and that she would go back with us. It is absolutely mind-blowing to me that my parents knew each other so well that something like that happened and neither of them gave up on each other, even if death did they part. Now, that is the love we all dream about; we think it happens only in movies, but hey, I saw it with my own eyes, and it is real.

I remember touching my father's face and saying, "Oh, your beard is so long," as he hadn't shaved in a few months, "but let me touch your face to see if you are really my father." He used to wear very big and heavy glasses, so that is how I knew it was him.

Mother cried so much, and Father just hugged us, saying, "I knew you would come back."

I do not know why I had the need, in such a beautiful moment, to say, "Daddy, they all thought that you died, but I was the only one who knew you were alive." I guess it was important to me for my father to know I believed he was alive and I still had a family. That night was very special for all of us. It did not matter where we slept or what we had to eat; as long as we were together, everything would be fine.

The next few months were very hard, getting used to everything that happened. Bombings happened constantly, people died, we did not have water or electricity, food suppliers only delivered once a week, and all the stores were closed. It did not matter if you had money; there was nothing to buy. Money was worthless. At that moment in life, I realised, at such a young age, that money was worthless and the only thing that mattered was our family was alive and together. This affected the way I saw the world and dealt with life problems, and it sure was one valuable lesson.

Months passed by. The war got worse and worse; we could hear people dying everywhere. Sometimes, attacks occurred a few times a day, during the night or anytime. Sometimes, attacks went on for hours, and all we could do was hide in the basement and pray that they didn't hit the building in which we hid. Spending so much time with so many different people, you became one big family, so our hiding and basement time turned into family time.

Parents talked about good times before the war started, and children sang, played board games, or did homework—yes, homework, because even though the war was active, schools stayed open for children who wanted to attend. Of course, I was one of those children. I loved school, books, maths, singing, and writing. So every night while we were stuck in the basement, I made sure everyone finished his or her homework.

One day while I was at school, we got bombarded, but that time, the sirens did not go off. That used to happen most of the time before attacks; sirens would then go off after the attacks started, and that meant you had only a few minutes to run, as fast as you could because that would mean the difference between life and death.

My teacher tried to keep us safe in the school's basement, but all I could think about was my mother running down the street to come get me. As you might have noticed in the previous story, my mother did not care if she died or not. So I lied to my teacher that I had to go to the toilet, and I sneaked out of the school to get to her before she walked through the falling bombs to me. I ran as fast as I could to get home before Mother left, but bombs fell everywhere.

Soon enough, I lay on the ground, too scared to move. I could hear the noise from the shrapnel and feel it fall all around me. While lying on the ground for a few minutes, I realised that my mother would be in danger, as I knew that she would still come for me in spite of the bombs. I got up and started running again. I closed my eyes, covered my ears, and ran as fast as I could. Home was not far away from school, maybe a kilometre, but it felt as if I ran for hours.

Finally, I opened my eyes, and I could see my mother running down the street towards me. I will never be able to explain that feeling of pure happiness but at the same time fear that I felt when those few metres kept us apart, when something still might have happened to one of us. I ran faster and faster and finally had my mother's arms around me. She started crying and yelling at me for leaving the school, saying how foolish and irresponsible that was, and she hugged me so hard. I was only seven years old, so I did not know any better. All I ever cared about was being with my family. It amazes me to this day how strong I was, the way I thought and behaved.

Not long after that day, my brother and I played in the snow, building a big snow wall so no one could hurt us—a silly little game that at the time made perfect sense because if we built a tall-enough wall, no one could ever climb over it and hurt us. I had a pickaxe, my brother had a shovel, and the way our game went was on a count of one, I used my pickaxe to break the ice and snow, and on two, my brother used the shovel to get the snow out. It worked perfectly for a while. We had great fun. But then all I could feel was warmth all over my face. Somehow on one, my pickaxe got stuck in the snow, and without even saying two, my brother got his shovel stuck in my head.

I did not feel any pain at the time, just warmth all over me. I quickly put a big ball of snow on my head and ran into the house, calling my mother to come down and help me. I was covered in blood, and I still remained calm. But when my mother saw me, she started screaming and quickly ran down the stairs and towards the hospital, crying and screaming for help. The hospital was located not far away from my home, and Mother ran very fast, as I was losing so much blood and she did not know what had happened to me. I just told her, "I will be okay. It does not hurt that much."

When we arrived at the hospital, after I told the staff what happened, they told my mother that because they were short on anaesthetics, I wouldn't get one. They would have to do a procedure while I was awake. My doctor told me if I did not cry, I would get some lollies to take home with me. Lollies—can you imagine what that meant back then? I was so happy; I could only think about sharing them with my brother. Of course, I did not cry. Once they started stitching up my head, I felt so cold I lost control over my body and fainted. I will never forget that feeling—as if everyone was shouting down at me and I couldn't move. I remember thinking, *Oh no. If I die, my brother won't get any lollies.*

I was discharged from the hospital that same day, as it did not have enough beds; the staff needed all the beds for injured soldiers. When I got home, my brother looked so sad, and he had cried all afternoon, but you can imagine his face when he saw the little bag of lollies. Our grandparents came to visit the same day and were able to buy me a chocolate, so all in all, it was a very exciting day for my brother and me.

When I say it was special that my grandparents could buy a chocolate, I mean that even though people had money then, there were no supplies—no chocolate, sugar, eggs, milk, cigarettes, or cleaning products. Months would pass, and every now and then, we would get some of the most basic supplies. That was one of the reasons why we had a little vegetable garden ten kilometres away from the house we were staying in. That garden was special to us, as it was just behind our home where we used to live before the war started. Every few days or once a week, my parents would go find a few things.

One day, I asked my father if I could go with him because I had missed home so much. I was seven years old then, and our home was the only happy place I knew. With a beautiful flower garden at the entrance, a veggie garden at the back, and a little waterfall on the side, our home was our paradise. During the war, everything was different—grey and dead. Streets stayed empty most of the time. All the shops were closed. There was no laughter. No children played. There was no life left—just survival. A long walk was ahead of us, but I did not feel afraid. All I wanted was to see my home and be reminded of the years of happy memories.

After hours of walking, we finally got home; unfortunately, nothing looked as I remembered. Most of the houses had been bombarded and were completely ruined. No one lived on our street anymore. We picked a few potatoes, tomatoes, cucumbers, and onions. It helped our family a lot, when the only store open in the city had no vegetables for us to buy.

Dad and I had a quick lunch and started walking back home. This time around, we had to use a different road, as it was getting dark and enemy lines were more active during the night. As we walked through the villages and saw all the abandoned houses and ruined land, we came across a whole family that had been hanged on a big tree in a backyard: a father, a mother, and three children. My dad tried to cover my eyes, but it was too late. The smell overwhelmed me. It looked as if they had been there for a few days. It was horrible. My dad told me to cover my face with my jumper and to be careful where I stepped. We just said a prayer for them, and we kept on walking. My dad let the police know about the case once we were in the city.

We still had a few kilometres ahead of us, so my dad said we should walk a little bit faster and stay lower to the ground, as a sniper kept an eye on that part of the road. We had to crawl in very long grass on the side of the road, and it terrified me. I don't know if the sniper or snakes scared me more. I started crying. I said to my dad, "I can't do it. I'm so afraid of snakes." I got up and started running as fast as I could.

Not even a minute later, I was his target. The sniper started shooting all around me. My father screamed for me to get on the ground and not to move. My legs shook so much I stayed still, and my dad crawled to me. He hugged me and said everything would be okay. We had to stay there for hours, deep into the night.

A few weeks later, my father found out from his friends that that night, the sniper recognised my father from their school days, and that was the reason why he did not kill me. I guess I was lucky. From that day onwards, I had to listen to everything my father said; otherwise, he would remind me about that incident over and over again.

That same summer, we had another close call with death. My brother and I were playing at the entrance to the house, which was closed off and made of glass, because it wasn't very safe to play outside. Mother was making lunch, and Father was shaving. Without any emergency sirens, the bombs started falling down, and the noise was deafening. All the glass broke, and the chickens that we had in our backyard got hit. The squealing was overwhelming.

I hugged my brother, trying to protect him from falling glass and the massive cloud of dust. I put a shirt over his mouth and covered his little head. We stood still. A few seconds later, our parents screamed for us and told us not to move; they were coming to get us. We hid under the stairs, hoping that no more bombs would fall, as our house was pretty shaken up. That corner of the house was the darkest one. I never liked it, but it was the safest part of the house. As we stayed still, we could hear my grandmother shouting our names. Poor Grandmother had seen bombs falling at the back of our house and a massive cloud of smoke, so she ran to see if we were still alive.

Once we were all together, that was all that mattered—lots of tears and hugs and reassurances that everything would be fine. We found out then that all our chickens were dead. Grandmother said that our backyard looked like a graveyard. Our chickens were so pretty. They were so fat, and their feathers were so shiny. We had looked after them well. They were part of the family. My brother and I played with them every single day, patting them and giving them cuddles. My parents never let us out to see how bad it looked. They cleaned everything up so we were at least spared of that incident. We didn't have eggs for months afterwards.

I remember one day, my mother waited in line for almost a whole day just to get some eggs, and she came home with only three. We were so happy, and she was so excited that she could make us breakfast with eggs in the morning. I will never forget that feeling of pure happiness and gratefulness. When morning came and it was time for breakfast, Mother baked fresh bread, and we had some canned food that we got from the Red Cross and, of course, our three glorious eggs.

Mother asked how we wanted our eggs cooked, and my brother screamed from happiness, "Fried, fried, fried!" Then I remembered my brother liked his eggs fried, my father liked his eggs fried, and my mother liked her eggs fried. I stood there in front of her and said that I was not hungry and that I would just like a few pieces of bread with jam. My mother looked at me and burst into tears. She knew how I loved scrambled eggs, and by asking that question, she knew why I had said no to breakfast.

Even to this day, every time I remember that morning, I try to understand why I could not say, "Yes, Mother,

I would like a scrambled egg." Knowing we only had three eggs, I thought if I did not have one, at least they would have one each. I did not mind not having eggs. I hadn't had any in years, so it did not bother me at all. Milk, chocolate, and nice juices were a dream. I thought one day, we would wake up, and the war would end, and we would go back to our perfect home and live happily ever after.

By then, our country had been in war for years. Somehow, you get used to the bombs and the fact that at any moment, you could die; you try to live life as normally as possible. Our hope that the war would end never died. One of the incidents that I will carry with me for the rest of my life happened one winter morning. I was outside my home building a snowman when bombs started falling everywhere. It was so loud and very scary. I lay down and did not move, with my head stuck in the snow. The noise overwhelmed me, and it felt as if the source was getting closer and closer.

I remember I started screaming as I thought, *This is it. I will get hit and die.*

One of the bombs hit our neighbour's house, and it had such a hard impact I sank deeper into the snow. A few seconds later, I felt something falling onto me. It felt very heavy, and it hurt me. I could feel it falling next to me too. I thought I got hit. When I slowly lifted my head, all I could see was blood—blood everywhere. Strangely enough, even though it was freezing cold, I started feeling warm. I was covered in blood. When I turned around, I saw body pieces all around me. I could not believe what I saw. I started touching my hands and legs to see if those were my body parts. I was in shock and absolutely terrified.

I looked around. There was no one on the streets, smoke was everywhere, and I was all alone. I remember trying to call my mother, but I had lost my voice. I could not move or say anything. I just stood there, wiping the blood off my face. As I stood there for what seemed like hours, I could only think about why I could not walk; I just wanted to go home. I felt completely helpless. And then finally a relief: I could hear my mother screaming my name. She ran towards me, grabbing me off the street. That was one of those moments you can never forget and that leaves a feeling deep in your body.

Later on, we found out our neighbour got hit by a bomb while in his house, unfortunately. I could not speak for a week after that. I remember my parents taking me to the hospital, and all the doctors said, "She is in shock. It happens. Let her be, and make sure she sleeps as much as possible." My family was devastated. Mother kept crying and hugging me. I just wanted to tell them I was fine, but I just could not say it out loud. I got up every morning to go to school, I did my homework, and I played with my brother, but I could not speak.

One morning, I got up, went into the kitchen, and asked my mother, "Is this war ever going to end? I think we've suffered enough."

Mother got scared of me, as it was the first time that I had spoken in a week. She looked at me and said, "One day, my love. One day."

That day came soon enough. Presidents of three countries signed the paperwork and divided the land, and that was it. Our city was given to the other side, and we had to move. Trucks left the city every day. People were fast to organise themselves and move out of the city as soon as possible.

That is when money came into play big time; if you had money and wanted to leave the city, you had to pay truck drivers way more than they would charge in a normal situation.

Weeks passed by, and we were still stuck in the city. It was so heartbreaking and very scary, knowing the date when we had to move out. There were not enough truck drivers for everyone. They worked overtime for weeks, driving for days without sleeping. It was hard on them too. So my father gave up hope that we would get one of them to take us out.

We had a car in the garage that hadn't been used in years. He told Mother to pack only necessary stuff, and we would have to leave everything else behind. I remember Dad trying to turn the car on for hours, and it wouldn't start. He asked his friend to come help him move the car and push it down the street in hopes that it would magically start the engine. A big surprise was waiting for him under the car: a massive stash of bombs, bullets, hand grenades, and military maps. My dad was in shock. His friends were confused, asking my father why he had that in his backyard. My dad knew only my brother or I could have done something like that.

See, my school had been abandoned for months, and every now and then, I had taken my brother there so we could get some notebooks or pencils, as I was afraid that wherever we went, I wouldn't be able to go to school, so I would have to school myself. While I collected school materials, my brother found a military hideout in the school basement and went there on his own, collecting all the weapons. It shocked us, as it was very dangerous, especially his moving all those weapons on his own. He was so little; they could easily have blown him up. When my dad asked my brother why he did that, he answered he was scared we wouldn't have enough time to leave the city, so we had to be prepared to fight the enemy. That broke my heart. He was only six years old at the time.

The car was broken down for good. We had no options but to pray that trucks would keep coming.

On February 24, two days before the due date to leave the city, my mother stood in line for hours to get to talk to a truck driver who was taking another family out of the city and then would come back in two days, the last day to leave. So many people were in line. It worked like the markets; everyone yelled how much they could pay. It was horrible. Ladies cried and begged for help.

After many hours, only two ladies were left besides my mother. A truck driver asked how much furniture they had to see if it could fit on the truck. When it was my mother's turn to speak, she burst into tears, went down on her knees, and said, "Please, sir, take all this money. I have no more, but just take my kids with you. Please, just take my kids. My husband and I will start walking, and if we live, we live, but at least we will know they are safe."

As I looked at my mother on her knees saying that, I burst into tears and ran to hug her, saying, "It is okay. We will walk together. We cannot separate, now that the war is over."

My father had a gun with four bullets in it during the whole war. He had it in case we got attacked during the night; Father always said he would kill us and himself, as he would never allow anything bad to happen to us. We heard horrific stories that the enemy made children watch their parents getting killed, they raped children, and they slaughtered animals, and all of that done with knives—horrible, heartbreaking, and unimaginable.

I do not know why, but that truck driver picked my mother. She did not offer the most money, but she offered everything we had. He took her off the ground and said he would come back in two days. He said we had to have everything ready to move by then, as it was the last day to leave and it might get messy. My mother burst into tears and kissed his hands and feet out of gratitude, respect, and gratefulness.

February 26 was our happiest day in years. We got everything packed and ready, and our driver kept his promise and came on time. We said goodbye to our city. Our driver told my parents that he had not slept in days and to keep an eye on him, as he had found himself asleep behind the wheel during his previous drives.

When our long journey to a better and safer place began on the morning of Monday, February 26, we were prepared for anything. It was so cold that day, –22° Celsius, and our truck did not have a heating system. To make it even worse, as we were leaving the city, the enemies were moving in. Some of them started throwing rocks at us, and they broke our side window, shouted swear words, and called us bad names. It really scared us, but once we left the city, we were safe again.

Our drive was very long. The driver was falling asleep and smoked so many cigarettes. We were very cold and very hungry, as we could not stop for a break because he was on a deadline. Forty kilometres before our final destination, he had to stop. He was so tired that he could not drive anymore. We stopped in a village, and he asked a few strangers to take us in for a night, as we were refugees in need of a place to stay. They were so kind. A lady served us dinner and gave us a bed to sleep in. I could not have been more grateful when they turned their heaters on and we got so warm.

Unfortunately, I woke up during the night and did not remember where I was. I was so scared, and once again, I had lost my voice and could not call my mother's name. In the morning, I felt so embarrassed; I could not believe that I had wet my bed. I was so ashamed I blamed it on my brother. As an apology, my mother gave the lady a beautiful lamp because we did not have any more money left. She was so grateful and gave us the biggest hug. People on that side of the country had not gone through what we had, but they were very compassionate.

One would think that the rest of our forty-kilometre drive would have been easy, but halfway up a mountain, the driver lost traction, and the truck had no breaks on a frosty road, and a cliff only a few metres away. It was like a scene from a movie. Everything happened in a few seconds. The truck stopped; then we realised we were going backwards. The driver started shouting, "Get out! Get out!"

To this day, we do not know how my father managed to jump out, get timber wedges from the back of the trailer, and put them under the wheels to stop the truck from sliding down the cliff. For years after that, I had a nightmare in which we ended up down the hill in the river. It is a miracle that we survived.

## CHAPTER 3

# LIFE AFTER WAR

Our first day in that little village, which we had to call *home* for a while, was more than we could have asked for. People approached us from everywhere, asking us where we came from and wanting to know our story. We met a lovely family that took us in for the few days until the place where we would live was ready for us to move in.

Now, let me tell you about our soon-to-be "home." It was an abandoned old primary school, completely rundown, with no glass windows, no toilets, and no kitchen facilities—a tiny sixteen-square-metre classroom for a family of four. The first three years there were the hardest. It was a horrible and miserable place to live. My parents didn't have jobs for a long time, so they started doing farmwork. Tending to pigs, chickens, and cornfields was their new way of supporting us, putting food on the table and getting both my brother and me through school. We struggled a lot and had limited food and clothing supplies, but somehow, we still remained positive and happy that we were alive.

Summertime was really hard. Growing up as a teenage girl, I looked forward to playing with my friends all day long, but I was stuck in a cornfield with my parents, trying to help them out as much as possible. You can imagine that other kids bullied me, but I did not allow that to get to me. They would call me names like *little farm girl* and *Cinderella*, and yes, it made me cry a lot. But I still kept doing what I had to do, as my parents didn't have money to pay for workers. But then again, some of my most precious memories come from those cornfields.

My father would lead us; because the rest of us were so scared of snakes, he would always go first. Then my mother would follow, and my brother and I would go behind them. We would sing songs, and my parents would tell my brother and me stories from our childhood before the war started. We had long days of hard labour, but it was worth it. At the end of each summer, we had enough corn for our animals and some to sell to buy wood for cold winters. For most of winter, the temperature would go below –15° Celsius.

I remember seeing only yellow for days. We had about four acres of land full of corn, and once everything was picked, we had to dry it and then handpick it off the cob. That was where the fun began. It was a massive job. My parents had a few friends to help them out. It was a team effort, as my mother would say. I will never forget the skin peeling off my little fingers and the pain for days and days after.

September was always interesting, with school starting and everyone talking about what they had done over the summer—stories about holidays, shopping, and having fun. I would always sit quietly, knowing that if I said something about how I spent my summer and that I was actually proud of helping my parents, they would make even more fun of me. See, I was very pretty and tall, and I had long hair, nice lips, beautiful sparkling eyes, and an out-of-this-world smile, so I got bullied for that as well. No matter what I did, those kids picked on me, but I did not care. I didn't try to fit in. I did not pretend to be someone I was not.

I was very poor; my parents lost everything, so they could not afford branded clothes, nice shoes, or those beautiful rollerblades I so wished to have. I prayed for them every single night. I finished my years five and six of school in one pair of shoes, two pairs of pants, two shirts, and a jacket. From above 30° to –15° Celsius, I still had to wear the same clothes.

The bullies got their share. Once I realised that they would not give up, I had to do something about them. So I became vigilant. I fought them on every corner. I protected my little brother and other smaller kids too. Now that I look back on my past, I feel so blessed I had such hardworking parents and a loving family to come home to after school. I know that those small-minded people never taught their children what respect and love are and how to value life. They bought their children's love with presents, teaching them to look down on the less fortunate.

Our living conditions were very poor, with no toilet facilities, no running water. We had to walk for hundreds of metres to get water for showering, washing dishes, cooking, and drinking. We still got help from the Red Cross with food and hygiene products. Later on, we found out that all the canned food we ate was actually out-of-date dog food, not beef, but once you've survived a war, having witnessed all those horrible things, canned dog food is the least of the things on your trauma list.

After years of living in those conditions, some unexpected things happened; my mother got a job as an accountant at a bank, and my father got a job as a sales manager for a local company. The government built a block of apartments for all refugees, and soon enough, we moved into our two-bedroom apartment. We finally had a bathroom and a kitchen. Life was great. We could afford to buy nice things and live a normal life.

I loved our little road trips to visit my grandparents during that time. Mother would always get us lots of nibbles, and Father would play our favourite music so we would sing for hours. We would spend summer holidays playing and enjoying quality time with our family; it was so lovely. My grandmother taught me everything she knew about cooking and baking. I was twelve when I fell in love with it, not even dreaming that one day, I would make cooking my career.

The last few years we spent living in that village were certainly some of my best teenage years. I spent the summers rollerblading. Mind you, I still didn't have my own rollerblades, as my father didn't believe in doing the same thing other parents did, but my best friend had some, so I would borrow hers. We used to play soccer and basketball and go swimming in the river. It was such a nice way to grow up. During the winter, we would go skiing in the mountains every day after school and come home after for some bacon onion sandwiches and lots of rosehip tea. It was absolutely amazing.

We finally started having a normal childhood. But then in 1999, another invasion started. That time, it came from the sky. Schools were closed, and once again, we found ourselves in the war zone. This time, we had electricity, so we could watch everything on the news. Every night, it would show affected regions, bombed cities, and people running for their lives. Once again, we slept in fear for our lives and were woken up by emergency sirens.

After a few months of horrible fear for our lives, the bombing stopped. Soon enough, everything was back to normal. Schools reopened, and people started going back to work. My father always said that we would have to move to a bigger city once I finished primary school, as the village where we lived had no life for a bright girl.

So as soon as I finished primary school, I applied to secondary schools in the second-biggest city in the country, and I got into a fashion design school, the first class to open up in the whole country. We had a few weeks to pack and say goodbye to our friends. My parents quit their jobs and gave our unit back to the government, and we moved to the bordering country. I found it very hard to say goodbye to all my friends I spent seven years of a very colourful childhood with, but we had to move in search of a better future, as my father would say.

Once again, we were emigrants, with no place to call home. One would think that this time around, it would get easier, but life is not about ease; it is about how you handle really hard times. And once again, I was a target, bullied and laughed at for having an accent. I have to say this time around, it only lasted a year, as I learned to adapt really fast so I could live in peace.

My life as a teenager consisted of studying, cooking, working, and taking care of my brother, as my parents had a convenient store and worked sixteen hours per day. That city was my home for five years before I moved abroad on my own. I love that city. Even to this day, just thinking about it makes me smile. The city itself is absolutely amazing, with a population of 250,000 people. It lies on a river and is a cultural centre of the country. I loved every minute spent living there, even the bullying part, as I felt immune to it already.

Those few years living there were some of my happiest. I will carry the friends I made and the memories we created with me forever. That was the city in which Cinnia was created. Cinnia became my nickname, because of my long, curly, messy hair. I got my father's height and my mother's heart. I worked on my appearance from inside. I wanted people to feel the goodness before they just saw a tall, beautiful young girl with sparkly eyes and curly hair. Everyone knew who Cinnia was—a good girl, an amazing daughter, and an outstanding student—and I was very proud of all of that.

I thought I would have a long, successful career and a happy married life with two children in that city. There, I loved for the first time. We were the same age, only ten days apart, and back then, I thought he was the love of my life. He was kind and thoughtful. He had a beautiful soul and the most amazing heart. I felt that kind of love that never dies.

By then, my parents were doing well; I mention that because it played a big part in the way I thought about and saw life at that time. My parents had to work hard and very long hours, but just thinking about them having their own business, as immigrants, was absolutely mind-blowing to locals. Finally, we had a very good life.

I guess I gave in. I gave in to nice clothes, bags, shoes, and perfumes. Yes, I did all the housework, cooking, and cleaning; I did my brother's homework; and I studied and at the same time worked in a bakery as a pastry chef, so I felt I deserved rewards for my hard work with all the nice stuff. And my boyfriend at the time was such a nice boy; he came from a nice working-class family. Moderate and with no plans for the future, he got kicked out of high school. Some would call him a *troubled boy*, but I loved him. He was far from a troubled boy—just a lost soul—and I felt I could help him, be there for him, and support him through life so he could see in himself what I saw in him. Even as a little girl, I always had big plans for myself.

I wanted to become a family lawyer, an accountant, a chef, or a writer. I wanted to study and do as much as possible to make this world a better place. I've never looked at people through their religion, their skin colour, or their language; war didn't affect me in that way. I only see the good and bad in people, but I still try to see good in the bad too, just to give them that extra chance.

My parents, on the other hand, thought differently back then. Just because my boyfriend was from a different religion than me, my father told me I could not see him again. It shocked me. My parents had never been racist, so why now? Of course, I continued seeing him, but soon enough, I started noticing so many stupid little things that bothered me about him, and I broke up with him even though I loved him. I think I hated myself and my parents for it for years afterwards. His face while he was on his knees, begging me not to leave him, haunted me.

To this day, we still talk to each other every now and then, even though we live on different sides of the world. It took a few years after I left to heal and to get courage to ask for his forgiveness so we could be friends again. I then had one of those moments in life when pure love grows into something way deeper and creates bonds that can never be broken.

# CHAPTER 4

# LIFE AS A WIFE

I got married when I was twenty years old. The beginning of our relationship felt like a fairy tale. We fell in love with each other over the phone, as he moved abroad after the war and we got in contact through our families. Our families grew up in the same city and knew each other from a young age. We talked for hours and hours every day for months, later writing each other every few weeks, and we had that young, innocent love. He wrote me poems and promised a world of happiness. Everything happened so quickly. A few months after he came to see me, we got engaged and applied for a visa to get me to Australia. Before I knew it, I was on a plane, leaving my family and friends, and five days after I landed in Australia, we got married.

I always believed that love is all you need to be truly happy, and that is how I saw our marriage from day one. But the different ways that we were raised played important roles in our young lives. He worked as a tiler apprentice to his father. They lived in a massive villa, living the Australian dream, and for me, all that was new. His parents very generously gave us a deposit for our home instead of a big wedding. So within two months, we bought our one-bedroom unit. It seemed I would live that Australian dream too, but unfortunately, the first few years of our marriage turned out to be the hardest years of my life.

I knew about my husband's love for drugs before I even went to Australia. He was very honest about it, but I believed that once we were together, and once he felt loved, his love for marijuana would fade. See, in Western society, drug abuse from a young age is very common, but for me, that was all very new. We had similar childhoods, coming from the war zone and living the way we lived, so I did not quite understand his depression and why he was still stuck in his childhood now that we were safe from it all. Depression is something that people hide, and anxiety is something that people learn to live with.

Little did I know he came from an abusive family and still hadn't healed from everything that happened to him as a child. Again, I thought my love would heal him and help him fight his demons, but I was wrong. Oh, how wrong I was, thinking that as a twenty-year-old, I was mature enough to help him. Everyone thought we had it all, a young couple in love, working and well respected, who had our own place. And then at night, our lives were a living hell. Years of abuse lay ahead of me, but I was too blind to see it, too proud to admit it.

He first hit me in his parents' house one month after I moved to Australia. His brother saw it happen and came to my aid. He told his parents too. It shocked everyone. I blamed myself, as I asked for cuddles that day and it was too hot, and he had just got back from a ten-hour shift at work. So no wonder why he snapped. We both cried after it, and he was so sorry. He said he didn't deserve me and that I should go back home. I told him that I would be more understanding and would not ask for cuddles all the time and that as long as we loved each other, everything would be fine.

The first six months in our own place were good, as we were happy and turning our place into a home. However, one day, he snapped again. I oversalted dinner, and that was enough to get the worst out of him. I was bruised for days, but again, I blamed myself for it. Not only did I fail as a wife in putting dinner on the table, but I also failed as a chef. That should never have happened, so that was my excuse for his behaviour.

I started working very long hours so I was barely ever home. My work was my life. My food was my happiness. Getting compliments from customers was the only thing that would make me smile. I stopped believing; stopped believing in myself, in love, and in life; and stopped believing in the good in people, but I never gave up hope.

Hope was the only thing that kept me going. I thought that one day, he would wake up and realise that all the things that he did to me were not right, and he would appreciate that I was still there for him, because if I left, he would have no one. But that never happened. Months would pass, and then he would do it again, just that time around, it would be more extreme. I felt like a punching bag, good for nothing.

Bruises healed, but words he used to hurt me would stay stuck in my head for years, and I felt so alone. I did not want to admit to myself that I was a victim of abuse, that nothing good was left in him. I felt so afraid of failure as a wife to make my husband happy. I kept thinking, *It will get better. We just need more time.*

And then one night, he just lost it. I was beaten up so much that I had a dislocated shoulder, my legs turned purple within minutes, my head spun, and I fainted. I tried leaving that night, but he did not let me; he took my keys and would not let me out. Police came. I blamed my condition on my diet, saying, "I fainted because I was hungry, so my husband got scared and screamed. That is why my neighbours called you." Oh, I felt so ashamed, standing in front of officers in my underwear. They knew I was lying, but they couldn't do anything to help me.

That was the first night I thought of suicide. He was asleep in the bedroom while I was in the living room. The walls of our home were covered in Coca-Cola after he threw cans at me, with glass on the tiles and mess everywhere. My head hurt so much, as that night, he had hit me very hard all over my head. I thought, *This is not a life. One day, he will kill me and go to jail for it. I might as well do it myself.* I cleaned everything and sat down in the dark. I thought if I cut my veins with a knife, I may not do it right, and I would not die. I thought if I jumped from the balcony, which was only the first floor, I might break a leg, and then what? *Oh, I can jump onto the highway and maybe jump in front of a car, but it's 2:00 a.m., and what if there is no traffic and someone else gets blamed for my death?* I thought.

So I sat in the dark, thinking of all the times I could have got killed in the war, and there I was, ungrateful for my life, living in a dream country with money in my account. But I couldn't live with someone who didn't respect and love me, someone who hurt me in so many ways, someone who could sleep in the bedroom after what he had done to me only a few hours before. My parents had not fought so hard to keep me alive just so I could take my own life and someone could call them, telling them I was dead. How could I ever be so selfish and do something like that?

So I just cried and cried until sunrise and then got ready for a long sixteen-hour shift at the restaurant. That was my safe, happy place. Once again, it was a new day.

Soon enough, he quit his job and became even more depressed. Fights became more frequent. It was a horrible and dark time. I did not know how to cope with any of it, so I worked as much as I could while at the same time going to college. Six months after he quit his job, he told me about his plan to move to another big city where we could start over again. At first, it seemed like a crazy idea, as I had a great job and I was available to cover all the bills we had, and running away to another city would not solve his anger issues or lack of respect for me. Before I knew it, though, we sold all the furniture and were on our way to a new city.

As you can imagine, nothing else changed, with the next few years of further unhappiness and more and more abuse. I slowly but most certainly lost my mind, questioning everything I ever believed in and the meaning of my life. Suicide was always on my mind. I was all alone, and it looked as if I was in a dark circle I could not get out of. Some days, he would be a nice, decent human being, someone I could have a family with and live a happy life with, but then out of nowhere, everything would change.

The first time I left him was five years into our marriage, and that, of course, was after a brutal beating up. He did not call to apologise or to tell me how much he loved me afterwards. He called to ask if I could come back and help him out with all the bills while he finished his second apprenticeship. I do not know why and how, but I said, "Yes, okay, I will come back and help out. Once again, I am here for you." And I kept my promise for two years. Meanwhile, every now and then, I saw hopeful glimpses that maybe, just maybe, we might work things out and have a great future together despite everything that had happened. I could see past all his imperfections and still see the boy I fell in love with. Deep down, he was very damaged, but he was a good person.

People say it's very hard to change, but I saw change as an opportunity for a better, happier life, so for me, it came naturally. I tried everything to the best of my ability and read so many books to help heal our relationship and move on, but even that did not happen. I changed to the point where I could not recognise myself anymore; I was lost. To this day, I cannot believe that after so many years of abuse, I still stayed with him. I can now finally admit to myself that I was a victim, I stayed for seven years with the man who made me cry my heart and soul out, the man who hit and abused me in every possible way, the man who blamed me for that abuse and somehow made me believe I deserved all of that when all I gave to him and his family were unconditional love and respect.

The day I left him for good, I still had bruises all over my body. He beat me up so much that my whole posture got out of place. I could not straighten up or walk properly. I had to see a physiotherapist a few times per week for the next few months just to get better, be able to work, and continue with my life. On the night of that incident, I remember thoughts of suicide became real again. Back then, we lived in the penthouse, and jumping off the balcony would have been the only solution. I remember the pain; it overwhelmed me so much that I had no tears left. It was only two years after my second back injury, which had had me in therapy and rehabilitation for more than a year.

And he had no mercy while bashing me. I could not feel my legs or my hands. Everything was numb, and that's when I knew that I could not keep up this life anymore. I could not live the life where I thought about suicide and took beating up like a professional fighter. To that day, I had had twelve concussions, and it was time to leave that life behind. I rented a little studio and took two suitcases with me. For the first time in years, I realised that I loved myself more than anyone else and that nothing mattered but my own well-being.

So I walked away with my head held high.

## CHAPTER 5

# LIFE AS A CHEF

My career as a chef started just after I finished secondary school for fashion design. I worked full-time in a bakery, mostly nights, getting all the pastries ready for sale in the morning, as I didn't want to put more financial struggles on my parents; I wanted to support myself. It was great. I loved it, learning something new each and every day. It was hard labour for the little-framed, skinny girl I was. My skin smelled of butter all the time, but it was well worth it, as I enjoyed creating delicious food, and it was my only source of income.

When I moved to Australia, I was in a very tough situation, as I didn't speak English. I wished to continue something to do with fashion, as that was the education I had, but I was advised that it would take a long time and I should stay in the hospitality industry. I started working in a dine-in and takeaway fast food–type café five days after I came to Australia. I had two weeks to learn everything and to work unsupervised, which I did, and I felt so proud of myself. The way I did it was very funny. I drew food and described it in my language to try to memorise it—all kinds of pastas, meats, vegetables, and sweets.

I guess I was lucky that my mother-in-law was one of the business partners, and I also worked with my brother-in-law and a few Brazilian girls who spoke Portuguese, and I could understand them, as I spoke Spanish. The fact that people ate bacon for breakfast in spring amazed me. Hash browns were something new, and the amount of butter people used in cooking shocked me. But I loved every minute of it. I learned something new every day, and it never felt like work because I enjoyed making delicious food and making people happy with it.

Two years in, it was time to move on. Days were swapped for night shifts, and I also started going to college to study for my Certificate III in hospitality industry, as that would help me get better jobs. Talk about challenging myself and my body. My workdays were fifteen to eighteen hours long; my food intake was my Red Bulls, cigarettes, and protein shakes. But I felt happy and like I was worth something. I was an amazing student and an even better chef, and that was all I needed to keep me going forward in the very dark times happening at home.

But my body couldn't keep up with my lifestyle. I was very skinny, and I was in pain most of the time. I didn't feed my body properly, and I never had time to rest up. So I decided to quit my job and get something with better working hours at a beautiful Italian place. My hours were 4:00 p.m. to 10:00 p.m. I still had college to go to, so I was still very busy, but at least I got home before 11:00 p.m. and had some time to rest. A few months before I finished college and got my certificate, my college went bankrupt and closed its doors, which left all the students in shock. We paid thousands of dollars for one year of study, and everything was lost—no certificates, no money back, nothing. It was a very stressful time. I contacted Trades Recognition to get my certificate recognised based on my work experience and also got a second job, as at that time, only one income was coming into my household, and I had to pay the mortgage.

Again, long days and long working hours took their toll on my health, but the satisfaction I got from cooking more than two hundred covers per night was absolutely amazing. I had great respect for my head chef. He was very harsh but so very inspiring. He pushed me to my limits, sharing knowledge every day with me, from how to improve my slicing and chopping speed to how to multitask while doing a service. To this day, I feel so grateful for every second I spent with him in that kitchen. Soon after I got my certificate, it was time to move and leave everything behind.

Sydney, oh my beautiful Sydney. I fell in love with Sydney the moment I got here. I fell in love with the streets, trees, buildings, beaches, parks, coffee shops, restaurants, and most of all, the oceanside. The ocean simply looks endless when you look at it from any of Sydney's beaches; it's nature's perfection.

Soon after moving and settling in, I started looking for a job, and it didn't take me long to get one. I loved it; meeting new people and learning new techniques from great chefs were all I had ever dreamed about.

My motto was "If I can learn something new each day and be happy, that is all I need." And then I started working in hatted restaurants. See, even though at that time I thought that was the right choice and it would be great for my career, it turned out that I just wasn't cut out for it. But I didn't mind the fifteen-hour shifts and the crazy amount of pressure because I served some of the best food on the Sydney culinary scene.

The amount of bullying they put me through and the fact that I was underpaid for the hard work I did still were not enough to make me quit, but I think the hardest thing for me was the drugs. Drugs are a massive part of the hospitality industry, and it is very sad that all those young people ruin their lives with them. I was never part of it, and I worked in quite a few hatted restaurants in Sydney. I guess I could not understand the reasoning behind it, and I could not understand why people felt so unhappy and incompetent doing their jobs without the influence of some sort of drugs. So I got bullied a lot.

Not only was I a girl in a man's world, but I didn't obey their rules. I wasn't a part of the team. I was so different, and how dare I do my own thing and not become a part of that dark circle. Cinnia was gone— the girl with curly hair, sparkly eyes, and hope for humanity was destroyed. I had my head shaved to zero, with only a fringe left. I got tattoos and piercings just to create this wall around me so all these people couldn't hurt me. For years, I kept saying to myself, *As long as I am learning, I'm not gonna quit. I have to keep getting better and better.* It was hard, but I wasn't gonna give up.

And then one day, it just hit me: I would never be able to change my industry, I would never be able to make the others see past drugs, and I would never understand why they did not feel happy to come to work, why they ran from themselves, and why they killed their bodies and minds doing it. It was never about food; it was always about politics. And that was the sad side of the hatted restaurant industry. So I walked away—away from high-class cooking, exceptional service, and high colleagues; away from the dream of one day becoming the best female chef in Australia.

I took a few days off and then started my job hunt. Before I knew it, I was running my own kitchen— my first head-chef position. The real challenge began there. I was so young and tried to do everything properly. From my previous experience, I learned that I couldn't trust many chefs, so I worked eighteen to twenty hours per day, making sure everything was done fresh and to the best of my ability. My Red Bull intake got up to four litres per day, followed by two packets of cigarettes, and I was so underweight. I dropped down to fifty-two kilograms.

Nine months into it, with only a few days off, I injured my back very badly. It just snapped. I was in bed for months, not able to move, on eighteen painkillers per day and little hope that I could walk or work as a chef again. I couldn't shower by myself or walk. I spent all my days lying on the floor, dosed on very strong painkillers, waiting to start with my therapies and rehabilitation program. The first three months of that were the worst of my life. I was in so much pain, and I cried myself to sleep. It was absolutely horrible. I gained fifteen kilograms, which made it even worse for me, as I had to carry this extra weight with no muscle support.

My therapies mostly happened in water, and I had a specific exercise plan that I did at home on the floor three times per day. Slowly but surely, I made some progress. I could walk for about fifteen minutes per day without passing out, which was a great improvement. But then the therapists increased my weight exercise, and that made my back inflammation worse. It took months for me to work up to lifting a one-kilogram weight.

The insurance company looked into getting me to study something else, as doctors didn't believe I could go back to the hospitality industry again. They wanted me to become a real estate agent, and all I asked from them was a little bit more time to get better. I saw all different kinds of specialists and also a psychiatrist; everyone made it clear that they were there to help me, and I felt very grateful for that, but also, they made it clear that I should probably give up my cooking dream, as working eighty-plus hours per week was out of the question. I struggled to stand for more than half an hour at the time. However, I wouldn't give up just like that.

In those times, I never thought I could follow through with the true meaning of mental strength. As I already had had a failed marriage and had experienced a hell of abuse at home and work, cooking was the only thing I had left that made me happy, something that would put a smile on my face all day long, no matter how hard life got. But those people who didn't believe in me said that I couldn't do it anymore.

It was heartbreaking. It took me thirteen months of hard mental and physical dedication to recover enough to get a doctor's permission to work part-time as a chef. Belief that I could do it and hope were my two best medicines; no amount of painkillers could kill my positive thinking. It was one of my biggest life changes, and I felt so happy and proud of what I had achieved. I stood on my two feet, surgery-free and ready to work once again.

My first working year after my back injury proved very interesting and challenging. I was at my prime as a chef, creating some delicious food but so limited by my back. I managed to work about fifty hours per week, and with the help of a chiropractor, I had some pain relief for most of them. This challenged me but was well worth it. My food had great reviews, and I could not have been happier. Newspaper reviews and photo shoots were part of it all; I absolutely loved it.

Throughout my career, many people approached me, offering their money to get into business with me, but I never saw myself as a business owner at such a young age. I still had dreams of seeing the world, travelling, and tasting the delicious food the world had to offer. My parents and brother still lived back home, so I liked the idea that at any moment, I could take some time off and spend it with them. I feared that once I had my own business, I would stop learning and growing as a chef and turn into a businesswoman. But a very good opportunity came along, and I became a business owner.

Everything happened so quickly and unexpectedly. I had two days to take over and reopen this cute little twenty-seater café. It was amazing. I created a simple but special menu. I did my own marketing and also all the paperwork. It was my little project. I felt so proud of myself. I had help from a few of my dear friends— chefs and baristas. Everyone came together as one to help me make my dream a reality. It was wonderful.

Each day, I had more and more returning customers, great feedback, and so much support from locals. I experienced challenges, with all the paperwork that had to be done and all the laws involved in it, but I learned something new each day, and even though I was under a lot of pressure, I loved it. By then, I was used to the fact that my life path was very hard, so it didn't surprise me when one Friday afternoon, seven weeks after I took over the café, I was advised that the whole purchase of the café was illegal and I had to cut my losses and walk away. Once again, I found myself walking away from something I loved. I faced massive self-doubt and became very depressed. It took me two months to get better and start cooking again.

Since then, I've had a few projects of setting up cafés that turned out to be successes, which makes me very proud. I love my food. I love creating it and making people happy with it. It feels like my life's mission. I had more than a year to reflect on the mistakes I made and realise lessons I learned from them, and for that, I am stronger, smarter, and wiser.

I look forward to my next little adventure with a smile and hope in my heart that this time around, everything will turn out perfect, just the way I have always imagined it.

## CHAPTER 6

# MIRACLES DO HAPPEN

The moment I started feeling love again occurred one spring night in the heart of Sydney. It was just about that time when I started kickboxing. My friend recommended a MMA gym as one of the best in Sydney, so I joined it and started going there regularly. I still had my head shaved and those protective walls around me, and I was still numb and lost, but I found myself on the right path.

That night, there he stood—a tall and handsome guy, stretching just before the class started. I couldn't take my eyes off him. His movement was so gracious it mesmerised me. They say our eyes are the windows to the soul, and that is exactly how I felt when I saw his eyes—that he could see my soul. I felt butterflies for the first time in years and was stunned by him. After the class, I went home, and all I could think about were his eyes, light blue but so deep. Every time I thought of him, I could feel his presence.

We trained together four times per week, and I could not wait to see him again. My friend knew already that he mesmerised me, so she introduced me to him. Oh my, I will never forget that night, or the way I felt when he shook my hand. It felt like a thousand lightning bolts striking me, and those eyes were even more magical up close. I nicknamed him from that day onwards *my magic man*.

We became very good friends. I enjoyed listening to him, and we could spend hours talking to each other.

I was in love. I loved every single thing about him. He was very smart; he was kind, caring, and thoughtful. He spoke in a way that captivated me. He knew most of what I had been through. He knew my life story, but most of all, he knew me. And sometimes, that scared me. I knew I was damaged and I needed a lot more self-work and healing in order to forgive, move on, and be happy. So the idea of someone else coming into my life and taking the walls down really confronted me. But I loved to love him. It made me feel alive again.

I started to act like myself. My eyes glowed, and it made me so happy. It took me a long time to give in and stop blocking everything good my magic man brought into my life. His energy was pure. I knew he was sent down my path to heal me and make me believe again. Our relationship was magical. We spent every day together. I felt like a teenager. He made me feel so special and put so much effort into keeping me happy. We had so many little adventures and made memories for life.

Soon enough, we moved in together. He was the one who helped me open my own café. He was the one who supported me through it all. He was the one who believed in me. But after I had to close my café, I was heavily depressed. I spent days crying and questioning everything I had done in my life up to that point, everything I had been through. I hit my emotional rock bottom. He was there for me as he always had been. He was my hero, my superman, my everything in life—the only thing that was real. But somehow, it didn't get to my head. I felt like a failure. I failed myself; I failed him. I was so disappointed in people. I doubted myself, and it didn't matter how much time I spent meditating or how many books I had read in the past. Nothing got me out of that dark place.

For the first time in my life, I felt so helpless and so lost. I knew I wasn't well but didn't see the light ahead; I didn't see the solution. I went back home for a few weeks to try to find my peace with people who knew me and had been there for me my whole life. But even that did not help. For the first time, I realised how lucky and happy my life finally was. My brother was still stuck in the same place, with no job or opportunities to get somewhere in life despite all his efforts.

My best friend tried to have a baby with her husband for a year, and they couldn't conceive. The pain I could feel around them was unbearable, and I could do nothing to help them. There were no inspirational quotes I could say. My other best friend still lived in the same little village we immigrated to after the war, with no jobs, no love, and no future. All my other friends from high school or primary school had their own real, bigger life problems, so I went back to Sydney feeling even worse than I had before leaving.

There I was, in a perfect relationship, happy and loved. My health got so much better; my back wasn't as sore as before. I finally managed to sleep through the night, but still, I kept torturing myself about how and why all of that happened to me. Because of this, we stopped talking to each other. We were not happy anymore. Nothing he said to me could make me feel better. I kept on pushing him away from me, yet somehow, I relied on him so much. I thought he would understand why I needed more time to snap out of it, as he knew me so well.

I moved out. Once again, I stood broken and alone. I ruined the only pure thing in my life. But this time, it was different. I hurt so much. He made me believe in something special, something magical, something out of this world, but it was gone just like that.

I spent two months crying, training, and drinking. I was so lost; I tried to understand my life, questioning everything I ever knew, asking the universe if this was my destiny. I spent countless sleepless nights trying to understand myself, my actions, and my life. Looking for an explanation, I asked myself a thousand times, *Why, why, why? Why me, and why now? What lessons am I missing in my life? What is life trying to teach me?* I felt so tired of everything—tired of my own thoughts, tired of hope, tired of life. Had I not suffered enough? And then I woke up. I was numb to everything.

My mother was very sick, in and out of the hospital, and my grandmother—the one who thought me so much about cooking, the one who past hundred-year-old recipes on to me, the one I hadn't seen in years—died. I cried for hours and hours, and then I didn't speak for a day. I didn't know what happened, but I felt reborn. I didn't question anything; I didn't cry, and for the first time in months, I felt at peace with myself. I remembered that Cinnia girl who left everything to go to Australia, the girl who survived two wars and was so positive and hungry for life, the girl who had dreams of making this planet a better place. That was my life, my destiny, and my story, and I would not give up on myself.

On Christmas Day 2015, I felt a need to go to church and pray. As I left after the Mass, there he was, my magic man. He looked at me and asked me to sit down with him. He asked if I was doing anything and if I would like to have Christmas dinner with family and friends. I said, "I'm not sure I could come." I didn't feel good.

I remember going home and my friend telling me, "That must be a sign. You are crazy if you don't go, and if you break down, you can just leave." Coming from her, that was very romantic. She was always the realist. So I went to his house, the place that used to be my home too. We had a nice dinner, and I stayed strong. I didn't cry and didn't break down.

After that, my magic man and I texted each other from time to time. I was setting up a business for a friend, so I stayed very busy with work and started doing twelve- to fourteen-hour shifts once again. We lived in the same area, so we would bump into each other all the time, and honestly, that was a little hard on me because I still felt butterflies every time I saw him. I decided to move to a different area so I didn't put myself through those situations until I had healed completely. For the first time in my life, it was all about me. I invested my free time in training, reading, and meditating. I spent time in the park and on the beach, danced, and spent quality time with my closest friends. I also used that time to grow as a person. I reflected on my life from a different perspective.

I've met so many people in my life and tried to help everyone in need. I tried to protect everyone I worked with; I gave them my knowledge and was there for them, no matter the situation I was in. Through the years, you realise that people come and they go, but only a few say thank you. Only a few stay, and you end up with a handful of people whom you can call *family*.

I realised that I am blessed to have a few of those people in my life, and we might not live on the same continent, but we truly love and care for each other.

After bumping into each other in a few pubs and separating for a while, both of us realised that the love we felt for each other was greater than any issues that we had. My magic man and I got back together, and I moved back in. I find it hard to define this kind of love; it's pure, it's magical, and it's different. It's that kind of love where you both feel the same things and you think the same way but you express yourselves differently, forming a perfect unity. I love him, and I love to love him.

Once again, my strength was tested. I felt sick for a few months, without knowing what was wrong with me. I started having a lot of blood tests and scans done, and I was put on hospital waiting lists to have more tests performed. One of my tests came back positive for fibroids; it found two of them on my uterus. I was in shock; having any types of tumours in your uterus is absolutely terrifying. I was advised that I had to see a private specialist and in the meantime adopt a fully alkaline diet and experience as little stress as possible. That was the time to wake up and do what was right for me. I stopped smoking and drinking coffee, alcohol, and energy drinks. I stopped eating meat, gluten, and dairy.

Those were the longest two months of my life, waiting on my appointment with a specialist. I had all the support I needed from my family, my friends, and my magic man. He made sure I stayed positive and knew he was there for me for good. I found it hard not to have bad days. Sometimes, I found myself crying and thinking, *What now? I'm gonna end up having cancer and not be able to have children. How will I cope with that?* I was in a lot of pain too, so most nights, I went sleepless, just thinking about every possible scenario. Hope, faith, and belief that I would be fine got me through the few weeks I waited, ready for my appointment and any outcome.

When I finally saw my specialist, she was very positive and reassuring. I had to go through a few more blood tests and wait for my results. On the 11th of November (11.11. angels number), my specialist called me, asking me to sit down. For a moment, I thought, *Damn, I am gonna die. I have cancer. Bring it on—another fight to the end, and I'll be a winner.* But that wasn't the case.

After she asked me to sit down, she said, "Congratulations, you are pregnant."

*Pregnant … pregnant … pregnant … I am gonna have a baby.* I started crying and said, "Thank you so much. I thought you were going to say that I'm dying."

She laughed and said, "No, this is your little miracle, and you are going to be a mother."

I had to go for an ultrasound so she could see if the baby was all right. I cried for a few minutes and then called my magic man. I couldn't believe that I was pregnant. He was in shock too but so happy and supportive, as he always is. My ultrasound showed our baby was healthy and growing. Suddenly, we became the happiest people on this planet. It wasn't just about us and our love anymore; it was all about our little miracle—a life-changing moment caused by keeping my body alkaline, a perfect environment for a beautiful little baby to grow in.

Since then, I've had a few more ultrasounds, and the baby is doing great. I could not be happier. I have experienced a lot of changes and developed a few pregnancy side effects, but I'm taking it day by day. And no matter what, our baby always comes first. So far, I have had no pregnancy cravings or any hormonal episodes; I'm trying to enjoy as much as possible.

My magic man and I are planning our future and getting baby's nursery ready. The house is a dream, which we will turn into a reality, with a beautiful backyard, a little flower and veggie patch, and plenty of room for our children to play.

The future looks bright, and what lies ahead really excites us. For all the ups and downs, we feel ready. We walk our path hand in hand, stronger and wiser. I could never have imagined this much happiness; I never imagined that my life story would be written like this, but I feel grateful for every single thing that has happened to me because these things have brought me to where I am supposed to be: next to him.

Miracles do happen. Hope is one of the most powerful forces on this planet, and believing in yourself is the key to true happiness. That is what I take from my life.

It's a baby *boy*.

# EPILOGUE

I can't wait to meet our little boy and welcome him into this world. I look forward to seeing him grow into a kind, respectful, smart, goodhearted, and generous gentleman, just like his father. I can't wait to help him make his first steps and speak his first words. I can't wait to cook for him and see his little smile while he tastes my food.

My love for him is greater than anything I could have ever imagined. I love his father with all my heart and soul, but this little guy is so precious I can't put it into words. My little boy is my blessing.

I could not be more proud of my magic man and how far we have come. He is an amazing young man, and he is my inspiration. He is the one who believed in me when I gave up on myself. He is the one who saw past my shaved head, dark eyes, and smile that hid the pain. But most of all, he is the one who made me believe in the magic of life again.

We don't know what lies ahead. But we can make sure that while walking our path, we create some of the best memories, which will last a lifetime.

Love and do good in life. Help people in need whenever you can. Respect others. Be an example of what you want to see in this world, and always stay true to yourself.

For everything that is coming, I am ready.